98.6 POEMS

Brick of Gold Publishing Company
New York
2017

Copyright ©2017 by Nate Fish

All rights reserved. This book or any portion thereof
may not be reproduced or used in any manner whatsoever
without the express written permission of the publisher
except for the use of brief quotations in a book review.
Printed in the United States of America

Fourth Edtion
ISBN 978-0-692-90180-9

Brick of Gold Publishing Company
New York, NY

thebrickofgold@gmail.com
@brickofgold

WITH

I am with the poets
The singers
The dancers and the writers
Especially the writers
We are the experts
You can have the businessmen
Take them
And make your own god damn country
You already have

EATING

Only a man who loves eating
Will admit that it is disgusting

A BASKET

How dare you
Be happy
At a time like this
Put me in a small basket with eggs in it
So I can be comfortable

PAIR OF NIKES

This is my life
And I am alone
And it makes me sad
And it makes me glad
I have a pair of Nikes
Stuck to my face

THE WRITER

There is nothing like the writer finding something good
No one is more serious, more funny, more sad,
more happy, or more cruel
Than the writer, writing

BANANA

Eating a banana only takes a minute

THE WORST

The worst have won
And left us to debate which among them is good
None
Is the answer
The best have lost
And left us only to remember

IF I HAD MONEY

If I had money I'd buy parmesan cheese
And a frozen dinner
I'd go to the art supply store and buy a bunch of scrap board and some ink
I'd get a twenty-dollar train pass
I'd go to a bar and buy a beer for you
I'd mail a statue to someone
If I had money, I don't know what I'd do
I'd buy extra batteries and a book
I'd pay my sister back and go record shopping
I'd buy groceries for friends and cook a dinner
With Tempranillo wine for Vern
If I had money I would go to a restaurant with a woman
And talk about how broke I used to be
I'd eat chocolate and pay admission fees
I'd buy some weed and cocaine
If I had money I'd buy a clothes rack and plain white t-shirts
Shoes, definitely new shoes
If I had money I'd take cabs around from place to place
How is it that some people have money
If I had money I'd give it away
After I got a blanket
I'd make digital pictures
I'd get my old mitt bronzed
If I had money I'd pay November rent
The bills
And get a surplus of household items
I'd get notebooks and go to the library
I'd have money in my pocket
I'd buy a pack of cigarettes
Gregg has money and he has two packs of cigarettes
One on the table
And one he probably forgot about next to the couch
If I had money I'd go to Chicago April 19th
I'd dress in old suits and maintain an impeccable appearance

WORK

Be hard on yourself
And soft on everyone else

THE PARTY

This IS the party

MY OPINIONS

My opinions appear
To the average man
Absurd

The irony, of course, is that I am correct

RICH

Someone forgot to tell this Jew he poor

PEOPLE

People like to like
Like other people like
So people like them
Like them

LARRY

Fuck you, Larry

TALKING

It always happens on my birthday
The winning lottery number
Someone almost jumps off a bridge
I don't want to dance too much
for a dollar fifty
But I can dance all I want
Some people can't handle it
A five dollar dick
The craziest Milos and Cleopatras know everything
And want to make everybody stupid and see the doctor
Before they marry
Does she drink wine
She may break a wine bottle over your head
Do you want to stay alive
Who wants to be a millionaire
It takes a long time
I've been a bachelor since
What year is this
Two thousand eight, seven, nine, seven, seven
See how long
The worst bachelor Guinness book
Buy her a drink
She'll wack you
I'm the doctor
Give me the gun
I'll shoot the motherfucker
It doesn't take nothing to make me dance
Did you see that birthday party they had
Somebody got killed murdered
I said search everybody they got guns
They got knives

A POEM FOR CARL

Make it now, Carl
While we can
Before something happens
And we can't make it anymore
Before someone has to make it for us
About us
Life's a bitch
We are lucky
Make it for them
Who cannot

I'LL FUCK YOU

I'll fuck you
Like a man

LISTEN HERE

Parents
Don't let your kids
Move to New York

PARADISE CITY

Unleash a cobra-snake
It's what they call amateur night in Paradise City
The negro equivalent to outer space

SMILE

The first time I realized I had a smile
Was on the walk to gym class
The first time I realized I had a smile
That makes people like me
Must have been soon after that

THE RAT HUNTER

Anything that moves is a rat
Anything that doesn't is a dead rat
A rat is as fast as
A piece of light
A piece of garbage
A flap
To scare a rat
Hiss or stomp

THINGS WE KNOW

How it feels to be tired
And how it feels to sleep
How it feels to be hungry
And how it feels to eat
How it feels to be hot
How it feels to be cold
How it feels to be young
And how it feels to be old

A STORY

I played ball
Diving, always
Bleeding
Dirty
Smiling
I made paintings
Hoping
Thinking
I wrote poems
knowing
I treated people well, too well, it feels like now
Friends and strangers
And in return I received nothing
The notion that you will be compensated for the quality of your work
And your actions
Is false
In case you happened to think it was not
You will be compensated in direct proportion to
Nothing in particular
To take but not give
To destroy but not care
To play but not really try
We made up a story that is not true
So then we made up another story

BUBBY

I never knew my grandmother was annoying
Until my sister told me she was

THE BIKE THIEF (Siddhartha)

He became a Dead Jackal
Stank of lies and ate fishes
Amongst carriers and dice players
The troubled stream of forms robbed him
False deity of businessmen, retreat
Every path
Them all
It is perfect

ART

Art is for white people

FLATBUSH LIFE

I was just reading the Trial by Franz Kafka
Ignore that I said Kafka
It's distracting
It could have been anyone
Anyways, I couldn't concentrate
I kept thinking
What if I die
And they find my computer
And all I have on it is this crap
How will they know it was supposed to be great

I am writing this so I am not forgotten

It was cold last night
I got home late
It was cold in my room
I remembered a blanket on the couch
A little green blanket but with the warmth of a large blanket
I went to the couch and looked through the copy of
Flatbush Life
The front page said

PAIR DIE IN FLATBUSH GARAGE BLAZE
Two men were killed when their attempts to turn a Flatbush garage into a heated shelter turned horribly awry, officials said. Police believe that the still unidentified victims perished when the papers and rubbish they had lit to keep warm set the garage on fire. Firefighters responded to the garage, which is attached to the basement of a home on the 1600 block of E. 21st street, near Avenue P, at 5:40 p.m. on January 19th and put the blaze out within minutes. The fire however, had already taken the victims lives. Autopsies were pending as this paper went to press. Officials describe the two men as white, possibly Russian males in their mid-forties to mid-fifties.

Horribly written
Tough fate for the Russians, huh
I told you it was cold
I said something to Chris about it being so cold
That homeless people would die
It didn't sound like a nice thing to say
But I was right
They weren't necessarily homeless I guess
You probably thought they were black
I imagined two black guys
With raggedy coats and hats
And gloves with holes
Like an Eddie Murphy movie
Real Hollywood bums
Skinny, rubbing their hands together
Talking about how cold it was
Then falling asleep on piles of trash
Burning and freezing, or freezing and burning
But it was two Russian guys
I assume they were drunk because they were Russian
I imagine them being somewhat heavier then the black bums, and
standing, passing vodka back and forth, happy
I imagined the black bums with some level of contentment too

RED LIGHTER

A red lighter
A red lighter
I was not expecting that at all

GAME BOY

I was playing my Game Boy
My mom reached back and handed me the envelope
I handed it to my dad
We were still in the parking lot of the hotel
I never stopped playing

BLACK MAN

A black man
Trapped in the body of a black man

THE MOVIES

I knew it was good
Because I shut the fuck up
For a second

YOU

In the morning you do dishes with songs in your head
You step from the bedroom with nothing in your hands
You are a hero and a jerk-off

POOR PEOPLE

It's the poor peoples' fault

A PHONEBOOTH

I don't want to describe to you
A phone booth
Not even to speculate
I only want to look at you and cry

THE POET

At least I am a great poet

SOMETHING THAT MOVES

I am drunk
A tree
Something that moves
Dead

THE END

It never ends
Then it ends

CHANGING

There is no such thing as changing
You are the same nice little kid you once were
Or you are the same mean little kid you once were

THERE IS A PLACE

There is a place
At the end of the line
Past everything
Past language
Past morals
Past science
Religion
Philosophy
And politics
There is a place
Past the planets
Where ideas wait to be born
Where love waits for us
Safely
There is a place
Go there

Go
Go
Go
Go

www.ingramcontent.com/pod-product-compliance
Lightning Source LLC
Chambersburg PA
CBHW062244300426
44110CB00034B/1924